ROBERT F. KANABY, Publisher
Mary E. Struckhoff, Editor
NFHS Publications

To maintain the sound traditions of this sport, encourage sportsmanship and minimize the inherent risk of injury, the National Federation of State High School Associations writes playing rules for varsity competition among student-athletes of high school age. High school coaches, officials and administrators who have knowledge and experience regarding this particular sport and age group volunteer their time to serve on the rules committee. Member associations of the NFHS independently make decisions regarding compliance with or modification of these playing rules for the student-athletes in their respective states.

NFHS rules are used by education-based and non-education-based organizations serving children of varying skill levels who are of high school age and younger. In order to make NFHS rules skill-level and age-level appropriate, the rules may be modified by any organization that chooses to use them. Except as may be specifically noted in this rules book, the NFHS makes no recommendation about the nature or extent of the modifications that may be appropriate for children who are younger or less skilled than high school varsity athletes.

Every individual using these rules is responsible for prudent judgment with respect to each contest, athlete and facility, and each athlete is responsible for exercising caution and good sportsmanship. These rules should be interpreted and applied so as to make reasonable accommodations for disabled athletes, coaches and officials.

2006-07 High School Basketball Simplified & Illustrated

Published jointly by the National Federation of State High School
Associations, Referee Enterprises, Inc., and the National Association of
Sports Officials.

NATIONAL FEDERATION OF
STATE HIGH SCHOOL
ASSOCIATIONS
P.O. Box 690
Indianapolis, IN 46206
Phone: 317-972-6900
Fax: 317-822-5700
www.nfhs.org

REI/NASO
P.O. Box 161
Franksville, WI 53126
Phone: 262-632-8855
Fax: 262-632-5460
www.referee.com
www.naso.org

ISBN-13: 978-1-58208-073-4
ISBN-10: 1-58208-073-9

Printed in the United States of America

Table of Contents

When the illustrations and statements do not give the complete answer, check the basketball rules book and case book for the technicalities. This book would not be simple if it covered all facets of the rules.

   Requests for basketball rules interpretations or explanations should be directed to the state association responsible for the high school basketball program in your state. The NFHS will assist in answering rules questions from state associations whenever called upon.

2006-07 Basketball Rules Changes

3-5-3 . . . . . . Changed the guidelines for headbands and sweatbands.

3-6. . . . . Added that a school logo/mascot is also permitted on the pants, compression shorts, headbands and sweatbands.

5-10-1 . . . . . The exact time observed by the official may be placed on the clock when a timer's mistake has occurred.

4-47-4,
10-1-5e New A fourth warning for delay was added for failure to have the court ready to play following any time-out.

9-2-11,
10-1-5c,
10-1-5d . . . . Changed the procedure for delay warnings to only one warning for any of four delay situations (previously three).

Signal Chart Established a new signal for a team-control foul. The arm is extended and the fist is punched.

2006-07 Major Editorial Changes

3-3-6 . . . . . . Clarified that a player with any amount of blood on his/her uniform shall be directed to leave the game until the situation is corrected.

4-10 . . . . . . Clarified when a closely-guarded count is terminated.

4-19-14 . . . . Clarified the definition of an unsporting foul.

4-34-1,
4-34-2 . . . . . Clarified the definition of player versus bench personnel.

5-11-2 . . . . . Clarified that during a 30-second time-out, no on-court entertainment should occur.

Points of Emphasis

1. Concussions
2. Uniforms
3. Time-outs
4. Intentional Fouls
5. Rule Enforcement/Proper Signal Use

Part 1

New or Revised Rules

The NFHS Basketball Rules Committee always keeps the following basic objectives before it:

- Fair play so that neither team gains an unfair advantage
- A balance between offense and defense
- Careful definitions of words and expressions
- Keep rules brief and concise
- Avoid exceptions
- Have simple statements
- Properly codify
- Write rules that are proper for level of play
- Minimizing risks to participants
- Use of fundamental statements.

These objectives can only be realized as long as the rules are administered as written and without exception. To set aside a rule which benefits one team or the other.

This simplified and illustrated book is a supplement to the basketball rules book and other materials which are designed to make officiating and coaching easier through uniformity of interpretations and rulings, and standardization of mechanics for game administration.

The rules are based upon sound fundamentals and axioms which make it possible for those studying them to apply certain basic principles rather than resorting to rote memory in the study and teaching of rules. Hundreds of administrators, coaches and officials have contributed to the logical development of the NFHS basketball rules.

The NFHS Basketball Rules Committee annually considers many items which were submitted as potential changes or revisions. The items which secured favorable endorsement are listed on the previous page of this book. The majority of illustrations in Part I show these additions and revisions. These illustrations are intended to answer the obvious questions which are raised in regard to the new rules.

When possible, some illustrations are presented to cover the "Points of Emphasis" identified by the committee. In some cases, a future rule change may have to be enacted in response to this problem area.

The illustrations found in Part II of this book have been edited to reflect any changes or clarifications as directed by the committee. Recent interpretations have been added to keep the contents current.

NOTE: Unless specifically indicated, all illustrations involve a two-point try and not a three-point try. When applicable, Team A always refers to the team in light-colored jerseys. Team B is always the team in the dark-colored jerseys.

3-5-3 Headbands and sweatbands must be white or match the dominant color of the jersey and be the same color for all team members. Sweatbands must be worn below the elbow and be a maximum of four inches.

3-5-3 Headbands and sweatbands must be the same color for all team members. Number 55 would be forced to remove the white wristband to conform to the colors of the other team members.

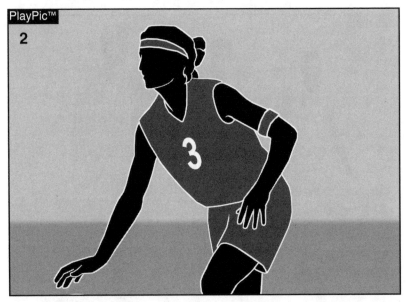

3-5-3 In (1), the wristband is legal as it is worn below the elbow is less than four inches in length. In (2), the wristband would need to be removed or adjusted to below the elbow before the player could participate.

3-6 A school logo/mascot is permitted on the pants, compression shorts, headbands and sweatbands.

4-47-4 A team shall be issued a team warning for delay when it fails to have the court ready for play following a time-out. It is one of the four delay situations when a team will receive a team warning for delay.

PLANE VIOLATION WARNING

INTERFERING WITH BALL AFTER GOAL

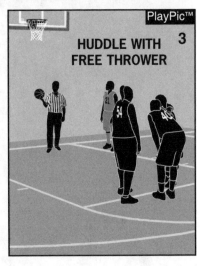

HUDDLE WITH FREE THROWER

4-47, 10-1-5 A team will receive only one team delay warning for any of the four delay situations. (The fourth delay situation, not having the court ready for play following a time-out, is pictured on the previous page.) Any subsequent delay in any of the four team delay categories will result in a team technical foul.

5-10-1 When the foul occurs with 2.6 seconds left in (1), the clock will be reset to 2.6 seconds in (2) when the official has definite knowledge. The need for lag time or reaction time by the clock operator has been eliminated.

POE No on-court entertainment is to be allowed during a 30-second time-out.

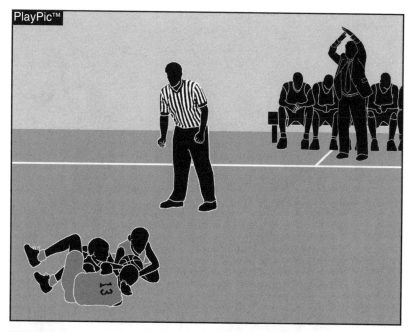

POE Officials should not grant a time-out until player control is clearly established. A request for a time-out does not guarantee that a time-out will be granted during a scramble for a loose ball.

POE Time-outs after a made basket should not be granted to the scoring team when the ball is at the disposal of the thrower.

POE In throw-in situations, fouling a player that is not involved in the play should be called intentional.

Part 2
Rule 1

Court and Diagram

The playing court shall be a rectangular surface free from obstructions and with dimensions not greater than 94 feet in length by 50 feet in width. Ideal measurements for high school competition are 84 feet by 50 feet. There shall be at least 3 feet (preferably 10 feet) of unobstructed space outside the boundaries.

The backboards shall be of any rigid material and either transparent or nontransparent. The front surface shall be flat and, unless it is transparent, it shall be white. Tinted glass backboards are prohibited beginning with those manufactured after January 1, 1995. The backboard shall either be fan-shaped or rectangular, with specifications as found in the rules book. The bottom and each side of a rectangular backboard shall be padded according to specifications. The backboards shall be the same size at both ends of the court. No logo, marking or lettering is permitted on any part of the backboard, backboard padding, or basket. The padding shall be a single solid color and be the same color on both backboards.

Each basket shall consist of a single metal ring, 18 inches in inside diameter. Each ring shall be securely attached to the backboard. Either nonmovable or movable rings are legal. The upper edge of the basket ring shall be 10 feet above and parallel to the floor.

The rules book also contains detailed specifications on the required backboard padding as well as specifications for moveable basket rings. Also listed is an organization to contact for information regarding court lighting specifications.

SHADOW LINE IS 1/4 INCH WIDTH →

← CENTER RESTRAINING CIRCLE AND DIVISION LINE MAINTAIN A 2 INCH WIDTH

1-3-2 Note Clarifies that the 2-inch division line may be a shadow line. A shadow line is a line designating the required 2-inch width by use of border or outline lines at least 1/4-inch wide, which lie within the 2-inch width. Border lines that are the natural color of the court are permissible. The area within these lines need not be one color, but the continuous 2-inch wide outline must be clearly visible to the officials.

1-12-1g The ball shall include the NFHS Authenticating Mark. The mark can be displayed in either format shown. A current list of NFHS authenticated products can be found on the Web site, nfhs.org. If an official discovers that the playing ball does not carry the NFHS authenticating mark, the contest is still to be played provided there is at least one otherwise legal ball that can be used. The official shall inform the coach that a report will be sent to the state association for their review.

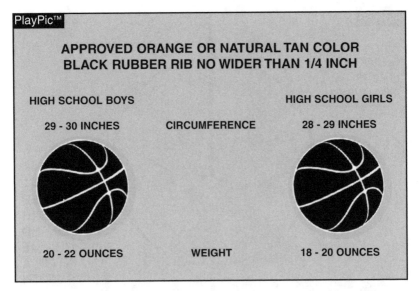

APPROVED ORANGE OR NATURAL TAN COLOR
BLACK RUBBER RIB NO WIDER THAN 1/4 INCH

HIGH SCHOOL BOYS   HIGH SCHOOL GIRLS

29 - 30 INCHES   CIRCUMFERENCE   28 - 29 INCHES

20 - 22 OUNCES   WEIGHT   18 - 20 OUNCES

1-12 The referee is the sole judge as to the ball's legality. The home team shall provide a ball which meets the specifications. If the home team is unable to do so, the referee may select one furnished by the visiting team. By state association adoption either a boy's or girl's size legal ball may be used for junior high school boys' competition.

14 FEET   14 FEET

HOME   SCORER & TIMER   VISITOR

X

MARKS   LOCATED OFF
2 INCHES   PLAYING AREA
WIDE

1-13; 1-17; 10-5-1 By state association adoption, an optional coaching box may be authorized. If used, the optional coaching box may be a maximum of fourteen feet (14'). An "X" is required on the floor in front of the official scorer.

Rule 2

Officials and Their Duties

The game officials are an important and necessary part of each basketball game. Officials must accept the responsibility of enforcing the letter as well as the spirit of the rules. Basketball officiating is not an easy task. The basketball official must be alert, quick and physically fit in order to be in the proper position to monitor the action of 10 players over the entire court. The game is demanding but it is also rewarding because the officials are vital to good game administration.

Good officiating is partially dependent on a thorough knowledge of the rules and the related material and use of the approved mechanics. Most decisions on the court must be made so quickly that they must come by reflex. The only way the proper reflexes can be developed is through continual study and practice. Basic fundamentals then become second nature, and correct decisions are virtually automatic. The individual who officiates in games played under the NFHS rules is extremely fortunate for there is an abundance of study material available. The high schools and their state associations provide training and proving grounds for many officials. A crew of either two or three officials may be used.

When an official accepts a game assignment, his/her responsibility is clear and well defined. The officials must make certain the game is played within the rules so that each team has an opportunity to exhibit its best. The responsibility for teaching the rules is that of the coach who must design offensive and defensive strategies which are within the rules.

2-1-2 It is recommended that the official scorer and timer be seated next to each other. It improves game administration when this is done. However, in some facilities it may not be possible.

2-2-2 The officials shall arrive on the floor at least 15 minutes prior to the scheduled starting time of the game. The officials' jurisdiction extends from their arrival on the floor until the referee approves the final score. When all officials leave the visual confines of the playing area at the end of the game, jurisdiction has ended and the score has been approved. Each official has specific pregame duties and responsibilities to take care of before the game begins. The use of either two or three officials is authorized.

2-2-4 The Team A coach confronts the referee immediately following the game. Even though the officials had left the playing court, all officials had not left the visual confines of the playing area. The technical-foul free throws will be attempted and if both are successful, an extra period will be played.

Rule 3

Periods, Time Factors and Substitutions

The substitution rule in basketball is extremely liberal. A substitute may replace a player any time the ball is dead and the clock is stopped. After a player has been replaced, such player may not return to the game until the next substitution opportunity after the clock has been properly started following his/her replacement.

A substitute who desires to enter shall report to the scorers, giving his/her number. Substitutions between halves shall be made to the official scorer by the substitute(s) or a team representative prior to the warning signal which sounds 15 seconds before the intermission ends.

At least 10 minutes before the scheduled game starting time, each team must supply the scorers with the name and number of each team member who may participate and also designate starters. After this time period has been reached, a technical foul is charged for not complying with either or both requirements. It also is a maximum one technical foul per team after this time period has been reached, for adding a name(s) to the team member list, changing a team member or player's number, having a player change to the number in the book, or a change in the starting lineup unless the change in starting lineup is necessitated by illness or injury or to attempt a technical-foul free throw.

Player uniforms must conform to listed specifications. These regulations have been adopted to assure ease of identification and to eliminate confusion for scorers, officials, players, coaches and spectators. If there is a question concerning legality of any equipment, the referee shall make the final decision.

3-2; 10-1-1 The name and number of each team member who may participate plus the names of the designated five starting players for each team shall be given to the scorer at least 10 minutes prior to the scheduled starting time of the game. After the time limit has been reached, a team is charged with one technical foul for failure to comply with either or both requirements. It is recommended the players' numbers be entered into the scorebook in numerical order.

3-2-2; 10-1-2 The scorer beckons the official and reports that all players of one team have different numbers on their shirts than those listed in the scorebook. The offending team is charged with one technical foul even though five infractions occurred. Either the numbers must be changed in the scorebook or the shirts must be changed to match the scorebook numbers. The two technical-foul free throws are administered to resume play.

3-2-2; 10-1-2 A substitute reports to enter but is wearing a number different than that listed for him in the scorebook. The coach informs the scorer that the substitute will not enter, thus avoiding the technical foul and penalty. Since no change had to be made by the scorer, no penalty is assessed.

3-3-1c Exception If any player has been directed to leave the game, an exception permits substitutes who have legally reported to the scorer to enter the game before the last free throw. By rule, players can be directed to leave the game due to disqualification, injury, bleeding, or an illegal uniform. All substitutes meeting this exception may enter the game until the official has beckoned the required sub onto the floor. At that time, any additional substitutes reporting to the table must wait until after the first of two or the second of three free throws to enter the game.

3-3-3; 4-34 A substitute becomes a player when he/she legally enters the court. If entry is not legal, the substitute becomes a player when the ball becomes live. A player becomes bench personnel after his/her substitute becomes a player or after notification of the coach following his/her disqualification.

3-3-4 The official stops play for an apparently injured player. Number 35 is actually not hurt and wishes to remain in the game. Since the official has not beckoned for assistance and no bench personnel have entered the court, the player may stay in the game and play is resumed immediately following the few seconds of delay.

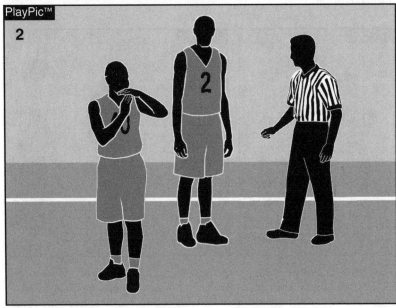

3-3-5, 3-3-6 In (1) play is halted because of the bleeding finger. In (2) a time-out is requested by No. 10. If No. 2 is ready to play at the end of the time-out, he may remain in the game. This also applies to a player with any amount of blood on the jersey; provided the situation is corrected.

3-4-6 Two of the players are not wearing undershirts while three are wearing them. Even though the length of undershirt sleeves varies from player to player, they are all legal as each individual player's undershirt sleeves are the same length.

3-4-6 Note Beginning in 2007-08, the home team shall wear white jerseys and the visiting team dark jerseys.

3-4-8 Team names and/or abbreviations may include initials. Horizontal lettering may be arched, but the first and last letters must be on the same horizontal plane, and the plane shall not be below a plane extending through the top of the number(s). Arched lettering below a number must have the first and last letters on the same horizontal plane and the plane shall not be above a plane extending through the bottom of the numbers(s). Any point on any letter shall not be closer than one inch to any point on any number(s).

3-14-5 Uniforms shall be worn properly. Shirt tails shall be tucked in as in (1) and (2); pants will be worn as manufactured. However, jerseys manufactured to be worn outside the pants are legal as in (3).

3-4-15 During playing action, No. 21's shirt comes out of his pants. However, as play continues, he does not tuck the shirt in even though he has had an opportunity to do so. In (3), the official halts play during the first dead-ball period and directs No. 21 to leave the game.

3-4-16 Permits a commemorative/memorial patch, not exceeding 4-square inches, to be worn on the jersey provided it is not a number and it is worn above the neckline or in the side insert.

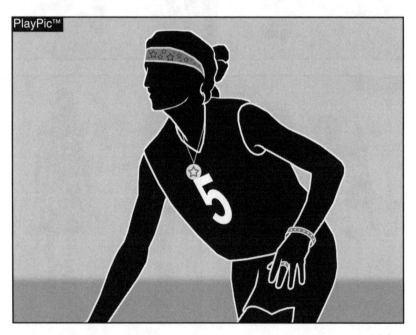

3-5; 4-34-4 The referee shall not permit any "team member" to wear equipment or apparel which, in his/her judgment, is dangerous or confusing to other players or is not appropriate. This includes the pregame warm-up period.

PlayPic™ 1

LEGAL

PlayPic™ 3

ILLEGAL

PlayPic™ 4

ILLEGAL

PlayPic™ 2

ILLEGAL

PlayPic™ 5

ILLEGAL

3-5-1 A brace, guard or cast made of leather, plaster, pliable (soft) plastic, metal or any hard surface — even though covered with cloth or padding — may NOT be worn on the finger, hand, wrist or elbow. If properly padded, hard substances may be worn on the upper arm or shoulder. Exposed hinges must be covered on knee and ankle braces.

3-6 One visible manufacturer's logo/trademark/reference or school logo/mascot is permitted on each of the items of player apparel as shown. The logo/trademark/reference may not exceed 2 1/4 square inches and not exceeding 2 1/4 inches in any dimension. No visible logo/trademark/reference is permitted on the shirt or undershirt. There is no restriction on size of logo/trademark/reference for warm-up apparel, including shooting shirts. Because these items of apparel are not worn by players in the game, the logo/trademark/reference restrictions do not apply.

Rule 4

Definitions

Coaches and officials have a tendency to overlook Rule 4, thinking that definitions are not as important as, for example, those situations dealing with various types of rules infractions and their respective penalties. Rule 4 is the most important rule in the book.

Basketball definitions apply specifically to basketball rules. A wealth of information is crowded into each definition. Some examples are:

1. **Alternating possession** is a method of putting the ball in play by a throw-in in all jump-ball situations other than the start of the game and each extra period.

2. **Bench personnel** are all individuals who are part of or affiliated with a team, including substitutes, head coach, assistant coach(s), manager(s), statistician(s), etc.

3. **A bonus free throw** is the second free throw awarded for a common foul, except player-control or team-control fouls.

4. **A double personal foul** is a situation in which two opponents commit personal fouls against each other at approximately the same time.

5. **Dunking or stuffing** is the driving, forcing, pushing or attempting to force a ball through the basket with the hand(s).

6. **Kicking the ball** is intentionally striking it with any part of the leg or foot.

7. **A pass** is movement of the ball caused by a player who throws, bats or rolls the ball to another player.

8. **Resumption-of-play procedure** is used to prevent delay in putting the ball in play following a time-out or intermission.

9. **A rule** is one of a group of regulations which governs the game.

10. **A try** for field goal is an attempt by a player to score two or three points by throwing the ball into a team's own basket.

4-1 Airborne shooter No. 32 has been fouled in the act of shooting. The defender moved into No. 32's landing spot after he was airborne. Two free throws will be awarded as the try was unsuccessful. The act of shooting includes the airborne shooter.

◄POSS►

4-3-3 A dunk during the warm-ups by No. 3 is a technical foul and results in two free throws for the opponents plus the ball for a division line throw-in opposite the table. The alternating-possession arrow is set immediately when the ball is at the disposal of thrower No. 4 in (2) as "control" is gained at that point for purposes of the alternating-possession arrow. The arrow is then immediately set pointing in the direction of B's basket. Team B will have the first opportunity to make an alternating-possession throw-in.

4-4-6 When the dribbler is unable to advance to frontcourt because of defensive pressure at one point, she may go into the backcourt and cross somewhere else. The 10-second count continues until the ball and both feet of the dribbler are touching entirely in the frontcourt as the ball then has frontcourt location.

4-5-2 Number 4 is confused and dunks the ball in A's basket. The covering official stops play after the dunk and credits the two points to Team A. Team B will then be given the ball for a throw-in from anywhere outside the end line.

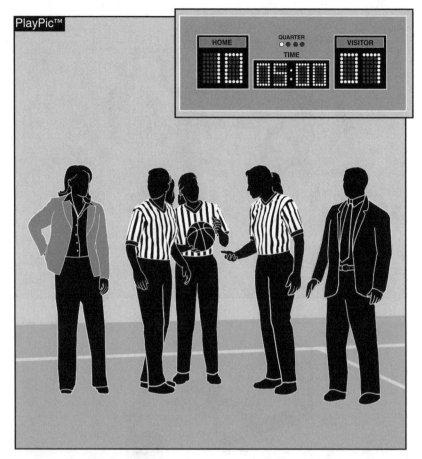

4-5-4 Both teams have gone the wrong direction to start the game. Even though considerable time has elapsed and points have been scored at each basket, nothing will be erased. The points will be scored as if the teams had gone the right direction. All fouls, violations, time consumed, etc., will stand and the game will resume from the point of interruption with both teams being instructed to go the right way. This procedure is used regardless of when it occurs.

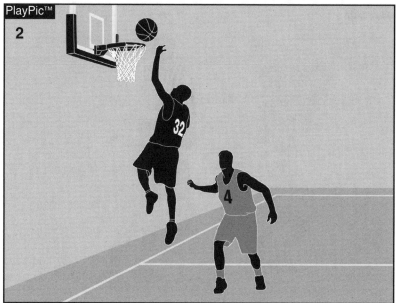

4-11, 6-7-7 Exception C A continuous motion foul can only occur when there is a personal or technical foul by the defense on a try. Continuous motion begins with the start of a try in (1) and ends when the ball is clearly in flight in (2). In a free-throw situation, a delayed call by the official would result when there is a foul by an opponent of the shooter.

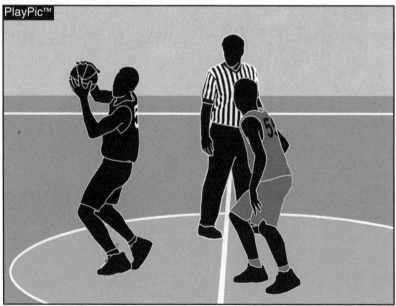

4-12-1, 6-4-7 If a jumper catches the tossed ball before it touches the floor or a non-jumper, a violation is called. The opponents will be awarded a throw-in and the arrow will be set toward the offending team.

4-12-2 This is an example of team control. It is team control during a pass between teammates. In situations involving deflected passes, fumbles, an interrupted dribble, etc., team control continues until the opponents gain control or the ball becomes dead. There is no team control during a jump ball or throw-in, or when the ball is in flight during a try or tap for goal.

4-15-3 Legal method of starting a dribble. The ball leaves the hand before the pivot foot is lifted. The dribble may be started by pushing, throwing or batting the ball to the floor. A dribble is ball movement caused by a player in control.

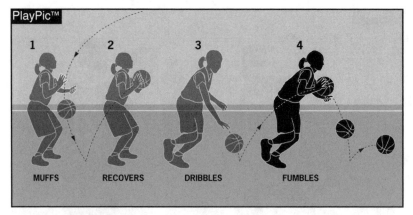

PlayPic™

1 **MUFFS** 2 **RECOVERS** 3 **DRIBBLES** 4 **FUMBLES**

4-15-4 The player muffs the pass, but she recovers and then starts a legal dribble. When she fumbles as in (4), she may recover the ball but may not start a new dribble as the dribble has ended. The term fumble denotes the ball unintentionally slipping from the player's grasp. The ball must be caught with one or both hands before it can be fumbled.

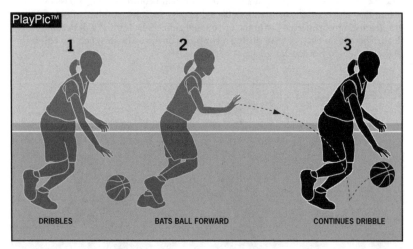

PlayPic™

1 **DRIBBLES** 2 **BATS BALL FORWARD** 3 **CONTINUES DRIBBLE**

4-15-4 During the dribble, the player bats the ball forward. She can continue the dribble as it has not ended. The distance the ball is batted has no significance.

4-15-4b In (1) the dribbler palms/carries the ball by allowing it to come to rest in the hand. The violation occurs in (2) when a second dribble is started. The proper signal is given to indicate the violation.

4-18-3 Number 21 dunks over his opponent and then verbally taunts him. The opponent retaliates and begins fighting. In this situation both players are disqualified for fighting. When the unsporting action of one player causes an opponent to fight, both are charged with fighting.

4-19-3 Number 41 is fouled on a drive to the basket in (1). The contact is judged to be excessive and an intentional foul is correctly charged in (2). Even though the defender was playing the ball, a hard foul is intentional.

4-19-6 Number 5 has the ball in his possession, and he is on the floor. Number 3 moves to get in position at the last moment; but he is stationary, has both feet on the court, is facing his opponent and is not moving toward No. 5 at the time contact occurs. Since No. 3 has obtained a legal guarding position, this is a player-control foul on No. 5. The official must be sure that the defensive player does not move toward the player with the ball and cause the contact as the defensive player is often moving from the side at an angle. Position is most important on this type play.

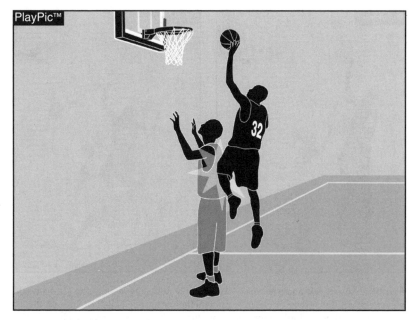

4-19-6 Number 5 has legal position on the court before No. 32 becomes airborne. The foul is on No. 32, the goal does not count if it is made because it is a player-control foul. A player-control foul causes the ball to become dead immediately. Number 32 is an airborne shooter after releasing the ball on a try until he returns to the floor.

4-19-6 This is a player-control foul. Number 5 obtained legal guarding position in the dribbler's path and maintained legal position. The guard is not required to have either or both feet on the court at contact after the initial legal position has been obtained. It would be impossible to move to maintain a legal position if it were required. If the dribbler gets head and shoulders past the guard's torso, contact thereafter is a blocking foul.

4-19-6 Number 4 is an airborne shooter when he fouls the defender in (2). This is a player-control foul. There can be no score whether or not the ball goes through the basket or whether the foul occurs before or after the ball goes through the basket. The player-control foul causes the ball to become dead immediately. No free throw(s) for No. 3. A throw-in for Team B at the nearest out-of-bounds spot follows.

4-19-7; 7-5-5 A5 sets an illegal screen on B3. This is a team-control foul. Team B will be awarded a throw-in at a designated spot nearest to where the foul occurred, even if in the bonus.

4-19-8a No free throws are awarded for a double personal foul, even through one or both fouls may be flagrant or intentional. Number 2 and No. 15 are disqualified from the game for fighting. The ball will be put in play at the point of interruption.

4-19-8b The four players who are fighting constitute two flagrant double technical fouls. All four players are disqualified. When a double technical foul occurs, no free throws will be awarded and play resumes at the point of interruption.

4-19-10 Ten minutes before the game is scheduled to begin, the scorer informs the referee that neither team has submitted a roster or designated starters. This is a simultaneous technical foul by opponents. No free throws will be awarded. The game will begin with a jump ball, as this is the point of interruption.

4-25-2 When the release of the airborne players try or pass is prevented by an opponent, it is a held ball. A held ball also occurs when opponents have their hands so firmly on the ball that neither can get control without roughness. An alternating-possession throw-in follows from the nearest out-of-bounds spot.

4-41-1, 5, 6, 7 The player taps the ball toward his basket. The ball does not rest in the hand, but the hand is momentarily in contact with the ball in order to give it direction. In a tap for goal the player attempts to direct the ball into his basket.

4-41-1, 5, 6, 7 In this illustration, the tapper is fouled when the hand touches the ball. This is a foul in the act of shooting and results in one free throw as the tap was successful.

4-41-5 The ball does not become dead when it is in the air on a tap even if time expires. A tap by a player toward his basket ends exactly as a try for goal ends and does not become dead if a foul occurs.

4-41-1, 5, 6, 7 The airborne shooter is fouled following the tap, but before returning to the floor. This is a foul in the act of shooting and either one or two free throws will be awarded depending on whether the tap is successful or unsuccessful.

4-41-1, 5, 6, 7 The player who tapped the ball is an airborne shooter and the contact in returning to the floor is a player-control foul. No goal can be scored whether or not the tapped ball goes through the basket.

4-42-3 The throw-in count is started properly in (1) when the throw-in begins. The throw-in count ends on release of the ball in (2). The count stops when the thrower releases the ball on a pass directly into the court. However, the throw-in does not end, and if stopped, the clock does not start, until the released ball touches or is touched by an inbounds player other than the thrower.

4-42-6 The thrower, when required to remain within the designated spot, may jump, pivot or shuffle their feet as long as a foot is kept on or above the 3-foot area.

4-44-3 This player's right foot is her pivot foot. In (2), the player lifts the pivot foot, and the ball leaves her hand on a try before the pivot foot returns to the floor. This maneuver is legal.

4-44-3 This player's right foot is her pivot foot. In (2),the player lifts the pivot foot, and jumps to shoot a jump shot. However, in (3), it is a traveling violation as the pivot foot returns to the floor before the ball leaves the player's hand on a try.

4-44-3 When the player, after jumping from the floor, drops the ball to the floor to avoid having the try blocked and then recovers or bounces the ball, it is a traveling violation. When she touches the ball, it is a violation as she released the ball to start a dribble with her pivot foot off the floor.

Rule 5

Scoring and Timing Regulations

A goal is made when a live ball enters the basket from above and remains in the basket or passes through it. Even though the ball is live during a throw-in, no goal can be scored if the ball is thrown into the basket from out of bounds without first touching a player on the court. If a player-control foul occurs before or after a goal, the goal is canceled. A goal from the field counts two points for the team into whose basket the ball is thrown. A successful try or thrown ball from the field by a player located behind his/her 19-foot 9-inch line counts three points. A goal from a free throw is credited to the thrower and counts one point for his/her team.

The scorer shall record the field goals made, the free throws made and missed and keep a running score. Personal and technical fouls are recorded. An official is notified whenever a player is charged with a fifth foul (personal and technical) or second technical foul. The scorer records charged time-outs and notifies the coach through an official when a team has used its allotted time-outs in regulation. These are but a few of the major duties the scorer must perform. A complete listing of duties can be found on the "Instruction Sheet for the Scorer" produced by the NFHS.

The timer shall note when each half is to start and shall notify the referee more than three minutes before this time so that the referee may notify or have the teams notified. The timer shall signal the scorer three minutes before starting time. The timer shall record playing time and start or stop the clock as provided in the rules. This includes a warning signal before the expiration of an intermission or charged time-out. A complete listing of duties can be found on the "Instruction Sheet for the Timer" produced by the NFHS.

5-1-1 After No. 4 releases the ball on the dunk, he becomes an airborne shooter. The subsequent contact is a player-control foul. The foul cancels the goal, even though the ball was through the basket and dead when the foul occurred. Team A is given the ball for a designated-spot throw-in at the out-of-bounds spot nearest to where the foul occurred.

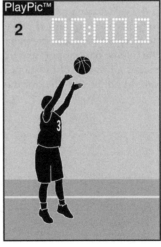

5-2-5 The throw-in is made with 3/10 of a second on the clock. The throw-in pass is caught by No. 3 and he then tries for goal. No goal can be scored on a try whether or not the ball is in flight on the try when time expires, in this situation a tap could score.

5-4-1 The coach has already been charged with a technical foul for failure to replace a disqualified player with a substitute available. It would serve no purpose to repeat the penalty or disqualify the coach. In this situation, the referee has support and authority to forfeit the game. Any act which makes a travesty of the game may result in forfeiture. However, a game should not be forfeited for the action of spectators.

5-6-1 The legal touching by No. 2 does not cause the try to end — thus the goal counts in either (1) or (2) as the ball was in flight prior to the expiration of time. If No. 2's touching had been goaltending, it would have caused the ball to become dead.

5-6-3 Exception A foul occurs as time expires in the fourth quarter. Team A leads by two points. In (2), when B5 misses the first free throw, the second free throw is not attempted as the winner of the game has been determined.

5-8-3 Only the players currently in the game or the head coach may request a time-out. The official shall see/hear the time-out request from either a player or head coach. If no indication is made for a 30-second time-out, then a 60-second time-out shall be charged.

5-11-2 In (1) the coach decides to call a 30-second time-out. In (2) the coach decides to call a 60-second time-out and the official properly instructs the scorer to also charge a 60-second time-out which begins immediately upon expiration of the 30-second time-out.

5-12-3 In no case shall successive charged time-outs be granted after playing time has expired in the fourth quarter or any overtime period. Team B's request is denied. This prohibition applies to one team or a single time-out by one team followed by a request by the opponents. In the case of expired time, the next opportunity for a time-out by either team occurs only after the clock has run in the overtime period.

5-12-5, 1-13-3 Time-outs shall be conducted within the confines of the bench area. Players shall remain standing during a 30-second time-out.

Rule 6

Live Ball and Dead Ball

Administration of the rules by logic instead of having to remember hundreds of rulings for specific situations is very often dependent on a clear understanding of exactly when the ball becomes dead and when it becomes live.

When the ball is dead, there are only three ways by which it can become live. These are:

1. When the ball leaves the referee's hand on a jump ball.
2. When, on a free throw, the ball is at the disposal of the free thrower.
3. When, on a throw-in, the ball is at the disposal of the thrower.

Unless there is continuous motion or the ball is in flight during a try or tap, the whistle always causes the ball to become dead if it is not already dead. The whistle is nearly always used merely as a convenient method of attracting attention to something which has already occurred to cause the ball to become dead.

Some rules fundamentals which apply are:

1. While the ball remains live, a loose ball always remains in control of the team whose player last had control, unless it is loose on a try for goal.
2. Neither a team nor any player is in control during a dead ball, or during a jump ball or throw-in, or when the ball is in flight during a try or tap for goal.
3. Any free-throw violation by the offense causes the ball to become dead immediately.
4. A live-ball foul by the offense (team in control or last in control if the ball is loose), or the expiration of time for a period, causes the ball to become dead immediately, unless the ball is in flight during a tap or try for goal. The ball also becomes dead immediately if the airborne shooter commits a player-control foul.

6-1-1 The game and each extra period shall be started by a jump ball in the center restraining circle. The referee will toss the ball for all jumps. Thereafter, play shall be resumed by a jump ball, a throw-in or by placing it at the disposal of a free thrower. Any two opponents may jump to start the game and each extra period. A throw-in under the alternating-possession procedure will start the second, third and fourth quarters and be administered by the referee.

6-1-2b The ball is at the disposal of the thrower when it is available to him. The official has properly started the throw-in count and the ball is live. While good judgment is required, anytime the ball is accessible to the thrower and all he/she needs to do is pick it up, the throw-in count shall be started.

6-3-5a Number 3 breaks the plane of the center restraining-circle cylinder after the ball is touched by a jumper. This is not a violation. Nonjumpers may move off the circle at any time. After the referee's toss they may change positions around the circle or move into unoccupied spaces.

◀POSS▶

6-4-1 Number 3 controls the ball then fumbles it out of bounds. Team A is awarded the ball for a throw-in because of the violation. The arrow is set immediately as Team B did obtain momentary control of the ball following the jump. This means Team A also gets the possession arrow and will have the first alternating-possession throw-in when the next jump ball or held ball occurs.

6-4-4 A held ball in (1) results in an alternating-possession throw-in for Team B in (2). The possession arrow is properly reversed when the throw-in ends. Team A will have the next opportunity when an alternating-possession throw-in results.

6-7-7 The foul by No. 4 occurs before the start of the tap. The foul caused the ball to become dead immediately. Number 4 tapped a dead ball. If Team B is not in the bonus, it will be awarded the ball for a throw-in at the out-of-bounds spot nearest the foul.

6-7-7 Exception a The goal counts when tapper, No. 4, is fouled after he taps the ball as the foul did not cause the ball to become dead. Since the tap was successful, No. 4 is awarded one free throw as he was an airborne shooter when he was fouled.

6-7-7 Exception a While airborne, No. 4 taps the ball toward his own basket. In returning to the floor, he fouls No. 5 who had legal position before No. 4 became airborne. The goal does not count as No. 4 is an airborne shooter on a tap. The foul is a player-control foul and Team A's throw-in will be from a designated spot on the end line.

6-7-7 Exception c This is continuous motion, and the try for field goal will count if made. Number 32 is awarded one free throw if the goal is made and two free throws if it is missed. The continuous-motion exception is the only situation when a foul before the ball is in flight on a try does not cause the ball to become dead immediately. The try for goal must have started before the opponent fouls in order for the continuous motion exception to apply.

Rule 7

Out of Bounds and the Throw-In

The ball is out of bounds when it touches or is touched by any of the following which are out of bounds:

1. A player or any other person.
2. The floor or any object on or outside a boundary.
3. The supports or back of the backboard.
4. The ceiling or overhead equipment or supports.
5. A dribbler who is touching a boundary.

A player is out of bounds when he or she touches the floor or any object on or outside a boundary line. The location of an airborne player is the same as it was when he/she was last in contact with the floor.

The ball is caused to go out of bounds by the last player in bounds to touch it or to be touched by it, unless the ball touches a player who is out of bounds prior to touching something out of bounds other than a player. When a player bats the ball out of an opponent's hands and it goes out of bounds, the player who batted the ball caused it to go out.

The throw-in starts and the ball becomes live when the ball is at the disposal of a player entitled to the throw-in. The ball shall be released on a pass directly into the court within five seconds. The throw-in, except after a score or awarded score, must be made from a designated spot. The privilege of running the end line following a goal or awarded goal remains after a time-out, after a delay warning on the opponents and if a foul or violation, by the opponents occurs when the end-line privilege is in effect.

7-1-1 Number 3, who is dribbling, comes into contact with an opponent who is out of bounds. Number 3 has not violated, and the ball remains live. Number 3 is out of bounds if she touches the floor or an object (not a person) on or outside a boundary. Number 5 is a player and not an object. However, if the dribbler touches a boundary line, the ball is out of bounds.

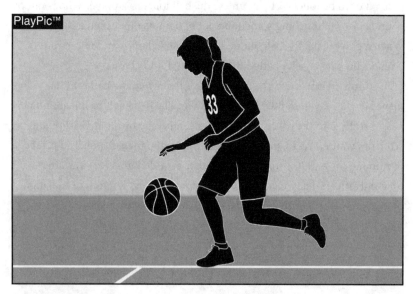

7-1-1; 4-15-5 A player who is dribbling (player control) and steps out of bounds during the dribble, even though she is not touching the ball at the time, has violated.

7-5-1 The final horn has sounded in (1) indicating the halftime intermission is over, but Team B delays at its bench. The official properly places the ball on the floor and begins the five-second throw-in count in (2). The resumption-of-play procedure is in effect to start the second half of play. However, regular delay provisions are in effect if either team has not returned to the court at the end of the halftime intermission.

7-5-5 A foul by B occurs before the free-throw attempt is in flight in (1). The lane is cleared. Since the free throw was missed in (2), the throw-in for Team A is from the spot out of bounds nearest the foul in (3). If the last free throw had been successful, the throw-in would have been from anywhere outside the end line. This is a team-control foul.

7-5-7 When there is a score, more than one player of the scored-upon team may be out of bounds outside the end line. Number 10 grabs the ball after the score, passes it to teammate No. 4, and is moving onto the court when No. 4 makes the throw-in. A player may run along the end line before making a throw-in following a goal or awarded goal. There is no limit on the number of passes which may be made outside the end line.

7-5-7 Goaltending occurs and a dead-ball player-control foul is committed in (2). Team B is awarded two points for the goaltending violation. Since the player-control foul in (2) does not result in a free throw for No. 5, Team A is allowed to run the end line because of the awarded goal.

DOUBLE FOUL
ON WHITE FIVE
AND DARK FIVE

SHOT

7-5-9; 4-36 The ball is in flight on a try by A2 when A5 and B5 commit double flagrant personal fouls. Both players are ejected, no free throws are awarded and play is resumed at the point of interruption. If the try is successful, the point of interruption is a throw-in by the non-scoring team from anywhere along the end line. If the try is unsuccessful, the team entitled to the ball under the alternating-possession procedure will have a throw-in at a designated spot nearest to where the ball was located when the fouls occurred.

7-6-1 Number 4 passes the ball from out of bounds outside the end line to his teammate in backcourt. This is legal as there is no player or team control during a throw-in and the ball does not have either frontcourt or backcourt location during a throw-in. Once control is established in backcourt, Team A will have 10 seconds to advance the ball to A's frontcourt.

7-6-3; 9-2-11 Penalty 3,4; 10-3-11 It is a technical foul in (1) when the defender reaches through the boundary plane and touches or slaps the ball away. In (2) it is an intentional personal foul when the defender reaches through the plane and fouls the thrower. If Team A has not previously been warned for reaching through the boundary plane, the foul also constitutes the warning being issued and recorded.

7-6-4 In (1), teammates have legally lined up for a throw-in using a tandem formation, and are not required to allow an opponent to take a position between them. In (2), the opponent may take a position between the players who have lined up side by side at a distance within 3 feet from the end line and parallel to it. If the Team B player desires a position between the Team A players, he/she must make the request before the ball is at the disposal of the thrower.

Rule 8

Free Throw

A free throw is the opportunity given a player to score one point by an unhindered try for goal from within the free-throw semicircle and behind the free-throw line. The try for goal shall be made within 10 seconds after the ball has been placed at the disposal of the free thrower at the free-throw line.

The free throw(s) awarded because of a personal foul shall be attempted by the offended player. If the offended player is injured or disqualified, his/her substitute shall shoot. Technical-foul free throws may be attempted by any player(s), including an entering substitute of the offended team.

The three spaces on each side of the lane beginning at the end line and moving toward the free-throw line are designated as marked lane spaces. The three marked lane spaces on each side of the lane are the only spaces which may be occupied. Except for the free thrower, all other players must either be in marked spaces or behind the free-throw line extended and behind the three-point line.

During a free throw for a personal foul, other than intentional or flagrant, each of the marked lane spaces adjacent to the end line shall be occupied by one opponent of the free thrower unless the resumption-of-play procedure is in effect following a time-out or intermission. A teammate of the free thrower is entitled to the next adjacent marked lane space on each side. No more than one player may occupy any part of a marked lane space. Only four defensive and two offensive players are permitted in marked lane spaces. If the ball is to become dead when the last free throw for a specific penalty is not successful, players shall not take positions along the free-throw lane.

SCORER & TIMER

VISITOR

8-1-2 Team B is not ready to play during a free throw by A after a time-out. Following the necessary signals, the administering official uses the resumption-of-play procedure and puts the ball at the free-thrower's disposal. Since Team B is not occupying the first marked space on each side. It is an automatic violation by B if the throw is missed. If B does violate in this situation, any further delay in occupying the spaces during the substitute throw would result in a technical foul.

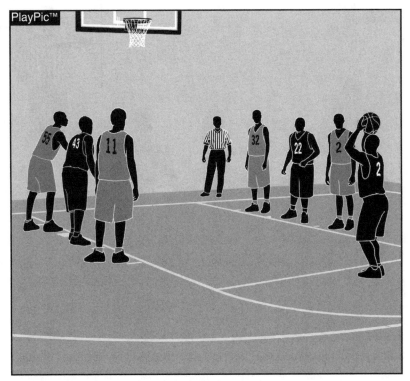

8-1-4; 8-1-5 If the ball is to remain live when the last free throw for a specific penalty is not successful, opponents of the free thrower shall occupy the lane space nearest the end line on both sides of the lane unless the resumption-of-play procedure is in effect following a time-out or intermission. Teammates of the free thrower are entitled to the second lane space. A team forfeits its right to any of the entitled spaces after the ball is at the free-thrower's disposal.

8-3 The free throws awarded for a technical foul may be attempted by any player, including an incoming substitute. The coach or captain shall designate the free thrower. Since an individual technical foul results in two free throws, each free throw may be attempted by a different player. If a technical foul occurs before the game starts, a substitute(s) may take the place of a designated starter to attempt the free throws.

8-3 The pregame dunk in (1) dictates the game will begin with the administration of the free throws. In (2), No. 11 who was not designated to start, legally enters to attempt one or both of the free throws. The replaced starter may not return until after the clock has run following the last free throw.

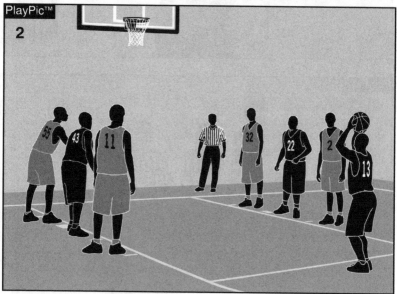

8-7 The ball is live in and at the disposal of Team B in (1). This is a continuous motion foul. If No. 2 was in the habitual motion of shooting the ball, the free-throw attempt counts and is succesful if made. The penalties are administered in the order in which the fouls occurred. Team B No. 13 will then attempt a bonus free throw in (2) as a result of the foul committed by No. 22 in (1).

Rule 9

Violations and Penalties

An infraction in basketball is simply an act of breaking one of the game rules. Whenever an infraction occurs, it is either a violation or a foul. It is often assumed that a violation is a minor infraction since no free throws are awarded. However, loss of the ball to opponents or awarding of points because of basket interference or goaltending can be very costly. Violations are of three types.

1. Free-throw violations.
2. Floor violations.
3. Basket interference and goaltending.

FREE THROW VIOLATIONS

This violation causes the ball to become dead immediately if it is by the free throwing team; but if it is by its opponent, it is a delayed dead ball since the ball remains live until the free throw ends. If the free thrower or his/her teammate violates, no goal can be scored. If the opponent violates, it results in a substitute free throw if the attempt is not successful. If both teams violate simultaneously, no goal can be scored, and unless another free throw follows, a throw-in is awarded under the alternating-possession procedure. If an opponent violates, followed by a teammate of the shooter in a marked lane space, the second violation is ignored.

FLOOR VIOLATIONS

A floor violation — like a 10-second backcourt violation or a throw-in violation — causes the ball to become dead. The penalty is the awarding of the ball to the opponents at the out-of-bounds spot nearest the violation. The more common floor violations include traveling, free-throw lane, backcourt, closely guarded, and those involving a throw-in.

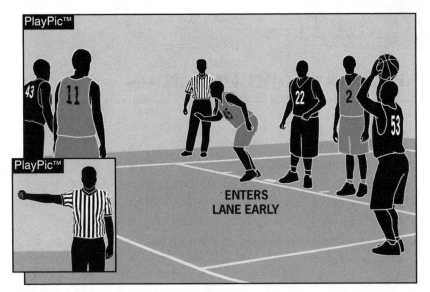

ENTERS LANE EARLY

9-1-9 The defensive player in lane one violates by breaking the plane of the lane boundary prior to the free-throw attempt striking the ring or backboard. The violation is signaled by the official and if the attempt is unsuccessful, a substitute throw is awarded. If the attempt is successful, the violation is ignored.

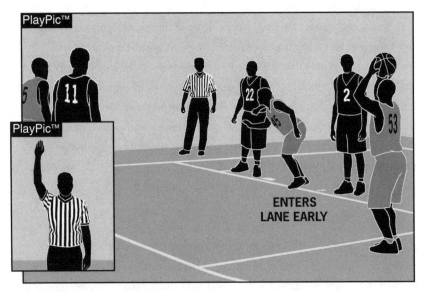

ENTERS LANE EARLY

9-1-9 A teammate of the free thrower commits a free-throw violation by leaving a marked lane space prematurely. The violation causes the ball to become dead immediately and cancels the attempt. Unless another free throw follows, play resumes with a designated spot throw-in by Team B.

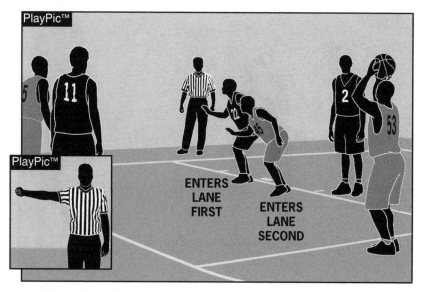

ENTERS LANE FIRST

ENTERS LANE SECOND

9-1-9 Pen If a defensive player in a marked lane space violates followed by a teammate of the shooter (also in a marked lane space), only the first violation is penalized.

9-2-2 In (1), No. 10 commits a throw-in violation when the throw-in pass strikes the floor out of bounds. In (2), it is not a violation when No. 4 bounces the ball on the out-of-bounds area before making the throw-in.

9-2-2 The thrower has complied with requirements by passing the ball into the court from out of bounds so it touches another player on the court who is either inbounds or out of bounds. Number 3 violates when she touches the throw-in pass while touching out of bounds.

9-2-3 It is a throw-in violation by No. 10 when a teammate touches her throw-in pass while the ball is on the out-of-bounds side of the throw-in boundary plane. The ball is awarded for a throw-in to Team A at the original throw-in spot.

9-3-2 A2 goes out of bounds along the end line to take advantage of a low screen set by teammates. A violation is called on A2 as soon as that player goes out of bounds. Team B is awarded a designated spot throw-in nearest to where the violation occurred.

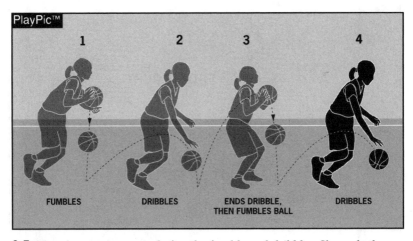

9-5 The player gains control after the fumble and dribbles. She ends the dribble and then fumbles again. She could recover the ball, but it is a violation in (4) to dribble again. A player is in control and cannot travel during a dribble.

9-7 The three-second lane restriction is not in effect while the ball is in Team A's backcourt or during a throw-in. The three-second lane restriction applies only when the ball is in A's frontcourt and only while Team A is in control as in (2) (also includes an interrupted dribble).

9-8 Violation. A team shall not be in continuous team control in its backcourt for more than 10 seconds. Team control was not lost by the dribbler when the ball was batted by the opponent even though the dribble ended. The count continues, and it becomes a violation when the count of 10 is reached. The count continues until the ball touches the floor, a player or an official, in frontcourt.

9-9-1 In (1), the player with her pivot foot (right foot) in the backcourt can pivot the left foot into the frontcourt and then to the backcourt in (2) without committing a violation. In (3), the player uses her front foot or left foot as his pivot foot and pivots into the frontcourt. However, when she now touches the backcourt in (4), it would be a violation.

9-9-1 The division line is in the backcourt. In (1), the ball remains in the backcourt even though the player touches the ball to the floor in the frontcourt. This is not a violation. In (2), when the player dribbles the ball while in the backcourt, it remains in the backcourt until the ball and both feet of the dribbler touch entirely in the frontcourt. There has been no violation. The 10-second count continues.

9-9-1 In (1), the player leaps from the backcourt while the ball has already obtained frontcourt status by No. 3. In (2), the player catches the ball in mid-air and lands in the frontcourt in (3). This is a backcourt violation as the previous location of the player who caught the ball in the air was the backcourt.

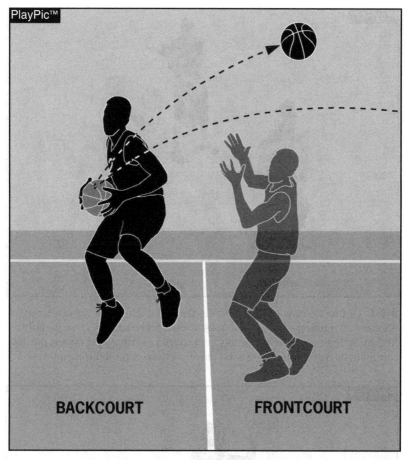

BACKCOURT   FRONTCOURT

9-9-1 The ball has not been to the backcourt, since it has not touched the backcourt or anyone in it. While in the air, No. 4's location is the frontcourt.

9-9-1 During a throw-in, No. 4 passes the ball to No. 10 in the frontcourt. Number 10 muffs the ball, and it goes to the backcourt. It is not a violation for No. 10 to recover the ball in A's backcourt as Team A had not established control in its frontcourt. There is no player or team control during a throw-in.

9-9-2 A violation occurs when a player causes the ball to go from backcourt to frontcourt and return untouched to backcourt if he/she or a teammate is first to touch the ball.

9-9-3 On a throw-in, if a player of either team is first to gain control while airborne, no violation occurs if the player jumped from frontcourt (1) and lands in backcourt (2). The same provision is in effect for both teams during a jump ball.

9-9-3 B2, while airborne, intercepts a pass from A1 to A3. B2 had jumped from B's frontcourt and landed in B's backcourt. This is not a violation. The provision is provided only to the defensive team and only to the player who secures control while airborne.

9-10-1a The trail official properly gives a closely-guarded holding count in (1) and then begins a closely-guarded dribble count in (2) when No. 3 begins to dribble. The dribble count continues as long as the closely-guarded situation exists anywhere in the frontcourt. The official should switch arms when going directly from one counting situation to another.

9-10-1b If players use the sideline or end line to keep an opponent from reaching the ball for five seconds a violation will be called. If one or more opponents are within 6 feet of the ball or screening players and cannot get to the ball because of the boundary line or the players, a closely-guarded situation is in effect.

BASKET INTERFERENCE AND GOALTENDING

Either of these violations causes the ball to become dead, and either may occur at the offender's basket or at the opponent's basket. The try for a field goal or free throw can never be successful if basket interference or goaltending occurs, however, compensating points may be awarded as penalty for the infraction.

If the ball did not become dead when the violation occurred, it would be necessary to credit the offending player with a field goal in the wrong basket when the violation is at the opponent's basket. It would be even more of a problem in the case of a free throw. The awarding or canceling of point(s) is easily administered after the ball is dead.

Basket interference can occur during either a field-goal attempt or a free throw attempt. It is basket interference to touch the ball or basket when the ball is on or within either basket, to touch the ball when it is touching the cylinder above the ring, to touch the ball outside the cylinder while reaching through the basket from below, or to pull down a movable ring so that it contacts the ball before the ring returns to its original position. If an opponent interferes, either two or three points will be awarded depending on whether it was a 2 or 3-point try. One point is awarded during a free throw attempt, if a teammate interferes, no points can be scored.

Goaltending applies either during a free throw, or a try or tap in flight. Goaltending is touching the ball during a field goal try or touching a tapped ball which is in its downward flight entirely above the basket ring level and has the possibility of entering the basket in flight. If an opponent goaltends, two or three points are awarded depending on whether it was a 2 or 3-point attempt. If a teammate goaltends, no points can be scored. Goaltending occurs during a free throw attempt if the ball is touched by an opponent of the free thrower after being released and while it is outside the cylinder. Goaltending by the defense during a free throw is a technical foul in addition to the violation. One point is awarded if an opponent violates.

9-11; 4-6 While the ball is on Team B's basket, a player of Team B commits basket interference at his team's basket by touching the ball while it is on the ring. The ball becomes dead immediately and no points can be scored. The ball is awarded to Team A for a throw-in at the out-of-bounds spot nearest the violation.

9-11; 4-6 This is basket interference by a Team A player during a field goal try by a Team B player at B's basket. Team B is awarded two points when the interference occurs during a two-point try and three points if during a three-point try. The official hands or bounces the ball to a Team A player for a throw-in anywhere along the end line nearest Team B's basket.

9-11; 4-6 It is a basket-interference violation for either the offense or defense to touch the net when the ball is on or within the basket. The violation causes the ball to become dead. If Team B interferes, Team A is awarded one point if it occurs during a free-throw try and two or three points in case of a two- or three-point try respectively. If Team A interferes, no points can be scored, and the ball is awarded out of bounds to Team B at the nearest spot.

9-11; 4-6 Number 4 touches the ball during a field goal try while it is in the cylinder above his basket and taps it into the basket. This is offensive basket interference. No basket. It is Team A's ball for a throw-in at the nearest spot out of bounds.

9-11; 4-6 Exception Number 4 secures a rebound while the ball is clearly outside the basket cylinder. As he jumps to stuff the ball into his basket in (1), No. 55 in blocking the shot places his hand against the ball while both the ball and the hand of player No. 55 are clearly outside the cylinder. In (2), No. 4 forces the ball and the hand of No. 55 into the cylinder. There is no violation by either player and a held ball with alternating-possession results.

9-11; 9-12 This block is legal as the ball is still in its upward flight and is not in the imaginary cylinder above the ring when touched by the defender. If the ball had been in its downward flight outside the cylinder and had a chance of entering the basket, it would have been defensive goaltending, if the touching had occurred with the ball in or touching the cylinder, it would have been basket interference.

9-12 Number 55 is goaltending whether it is a tap or try at B's basket. There is no difference in a tap or try as it applies to goaltending. The offended team is awarded two points on a two-point try and three points on a three-point try. Goaltending cannot occur on a field-goal attempt unless the ball has a chance of entering the basket in flight.

9-13 A violation in both (1) and (2). In (1), the violation does not cause the ball to become dead until the try is made or missed, then the violation is penalized. If the violation had been by the offense while the try was in flight, the ball would have been dead immediately. In (2), the ball is dead immediately. If contact occurs it would be either a player-control, intentional or flagrant foul.

Rule 10

Fouls and Penalties

Personal fouls involve contact during a live ball, except when committed by or on an airborne shooter. Technical fouls do not normally involve contact, but generally occur during a dead-ball period with the clock stopped.

The penalty for a foul is usually the awarding of one, two or three unhindered free throws and/or the ball for a throw-in to a player of the offended team. Penalties for fouls also include the offender being charged with the foul in the scorebook. Disqualification results upon being charged with a flagrant foul, a fifth foul or second technical foul.

PENALTY TECHNICAL FOUL: Specific infractions may be committed by a team, player, substitute, bench personnel or coach.

The penalty for a single technical foul is two free throws plus the ball for a throw-in at the division line opposite the table. If the foul is flagrant, the offender is disqualified. A technical on bench personnel for poor conduct carries not only the two free throw penalty but in addition all such "bench" fouls are charged to the offender and also charged indirectly to the head coach. The second technical charged to a player, team member or any bench personnel other than head coach results in disqualification. The third technical or the second technical charged directly to the head coach results in disqualification.

If a player, team member or other bench personnel commits a flagrant foul, the offender is disqualified to the bench. The same disqualification of a coach or adult bench personnel results in ejection from the building, or the offender must go to the team's locker room.

PENALTY PERSONAL FOUL: Offender is charged with one foul, and if it is his/her fifth foul (personal and technical), or if it is flagrant, he or she is disqualified. The offended player is awarded free throws as follows:

Summary of Penalties for All Fouls

The offended player or team is awarded the following:

1. No free throws:
   a. For each common foul before the bonus rule is in effect.
   b. For a player-control or team-control foul.
   c. For double personal or technical fouls (point of interruption).
   d. For simultaneous personal or technical fouls by opponents (point of interruption).
   e. After time has expired for the fourth quarter (or extra period), unless the point(s) would affect the outcome of the game.

   NOTE: If one or both fouls of a double personal foul are flagrant, no free throws are awarded. Any player who commits a flagrant foul is disqualified.

2. One free throw if fouled in the act of shooting and two- or three-point try or tap is successful.

3. Bonus free throw:
   a. For seventh, eighth and ninth team foul each half, if first free throw is successful.
   b. Beginning with 10th team foul each half whether or not first free throw is successful.

4. Two free throws if intentional or flagrant, plus ball for throw-in.

5. Fouled in act of shooting and try or tap is unsuccessful:
   a. Two free throws on two-point try or tap.
   b. Three free throws on three-point try or tap.

   Plus ball for throw-in if intentional or flagrant.

6. Multiple Foul:
   a. One free throw for each foul:
      (1) No try involved.
      (2) Successful or unsuccessful two-point try or tap.
      (3) Successful three-point try or tap.

b. Two free throws for each foul:

  (1) Intentional or flagrant foul.

  (2) Unsuccessful three-point try or tap.

  Plus ball for throw-in if intentional or flagrant.

NOTE: If one or both fouls of a multiple foul are flagrant, two free throws are awarded for each flagrant foul. Any player who commits a flagrant foul is disqualified.

7. In case of a false double foul or a false multiple foul, each foul carries its own penalty.

8. Fighting:

  a. Players on the court:

     (1) Corresponding number from each team - double flagrant fouls, all participants are disqualified, no free throws are awarded, ball is put in play at the point of interruption.

     (2) Numbers of participants are not corresponding - Flagrant fouls and disqualification for all participants, two free throws are awarded for the offended team for each additional player, offended team awarded a division line throw in.

  b. Bench personnel leaving bench area during a fight or when a fight may break out:

     (1) Do NOT participate in the fight — all players leaving bench are assessed flagrant fouls and disqualified, the head coach is assessed a maximum of one indirect technical foul (regardless of the number leaving the bench). If the number of each team's offenders is corresponding, no free throws are awarded, and the ball is put in play at the point of interruption. If the number of each team's offenders is unequal, a maximum of two free throws are awarded the offended team, followed by a division line throw-in opposite the table.

     (2) Participate in the fight — all participants are assessed flagrant fouls and disqualified. The head coach is assessed one indirect technical foul for each bench player participating in the fight. If the number of each team's participants is corresponding, no free

throws are awarded, and the ball is put in play by the alternating-possession procedure opposite the table. If the number of each team's participants is unequal, two free throws are awarded the offended team for each additional player, followed by a division line throw-in opposite the table.

NOTE: All fouls (except an indirect technical foul charged to the head coach) count toward the team's foul count in the half.

10-1-3 The coach is using a cellular phone at courtside for coaching purposes. This is an example of an item which is not permitted. A technical foul is charged to the offending team for such infractions.

10-1-5c The official is ready to administer the second free throw, but three Team B players are huddling in the lane. In (2), the official properly instructs the scorer to record a team warning for delay. The warning is then announced to the coach. If Team B is issued another team warning for any type of delay, it will result in a technical foul.

10-2-2 Number 4 runs onto the court without being beckoned by an official, while the ball is live. The penalty for this infraction is a technical foul. If the official fails to detect the illegal entry and it is detected by the scorer, he or she may call it to the official's attention. When this error occurs and it is not immediately penalized, it may be corrected, provided it is recognized before the ball becomes live following the first dead ball after the infraction occurred.

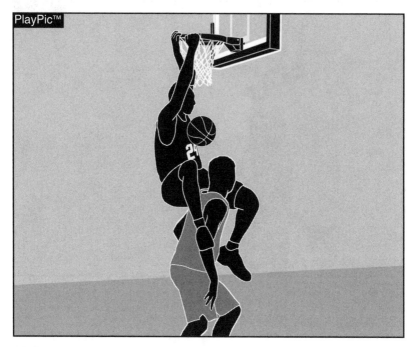

10-3-5 Exception Any player may grasp the basket to prevent possible injury. In the case shown, No. 24 is not penalized for grasping the ring to prevent injury to himself or to the defender. However, if such grasping causes basket interference, the interference is penalized.

10-3-6 The purpose of the rule is to penalize intentional or deliberate contact with the backboard with a technical foul. Contact that occurs incidentally in playing the game is permitted.

10-3-6 A player shall not: 1) place a hand on the backboard or ring to gain an advantage; or 2) intentionally slap or strike the backboard or cause the ring to vibrate, while a try or tap is in flight or is touching the backboard or is in the basket or cylinder above the basket.

10-3-10 Penalty In (1), No. 2 commits a flagrant technical foul for fighting. In (2), he is disqualified and directed to go to Team B's bench. In (3), No. 2 remains under the supervision of the coach and jurisdiction of the officials.

10-3-12; 9-2-11 Penalty 3 A player who reaches through the throw-in boundary plane and touches or dislodges the ball commits a technical foul whether or not a throw-in plane warning had been given previously. This specific act is a player technical foul. The offended team will receive two free throws and the ball for a division-line throw-in.

10-5-1 The bench-decorum rule is in effect by state association adoption. When the coaching box is not in effect, coaches are also restricted in their actions.

10-5-3 The timer shall start the 30-second clock immediately when the official notifies him/her to do so. The coach has 30 seconds to replace the disqualified player without penalty.

10 Penalty 4 Number 5 is charged with a flagrant personal foul in (1) and is disqualified in (2). Number 20 is awarded two free throws whether or not the goal was successful. Players are not allowed in spaces along the lane during the free throws. In addition, Team B is awarded the ball for a throw-in at the out-of-bounds spot nearest to the foul.

10-6 Rough play must diminish. Excessive actions when boxing out, cutting off and screening opponents must be eliminated. Coaches must not teach rough tactics and officials must call the infraction when it occurs.

10-6 Number 32 drives for the basket and takes off for a jump shot. Number 20 moves under the airborne shooter. The airborne shooter is in the act of shooting until he returns to the floor. When No. 20 moves into the path of an airborne shooter, it results in a foul against a player in the act of shooting. If the try is successful, one free throw is awarded. If the try is unsuccessful, two free throws are awarded.

10-6-1 Number 5 is blocking No. 12 when she illegally contacts her with her arms in an effort to obstruct movement. A player may not impede the progress of an opponent by extending an arm, shoulder, hip, or knee, or by bending the body into an abnormal position.

10-6-1 This is a player-control foul on No. 50 in (2). Number 33 has obtained a legal position and does not have to move from it. The contact is caused by No. 50 getting into position for a shot. Number 33 is entitled to her vertical space.

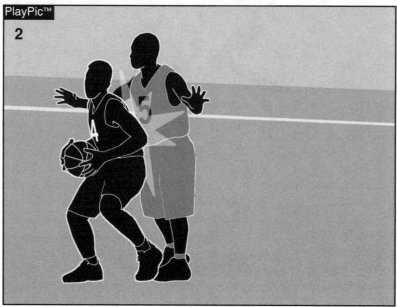

10-6-1 In (1), both players are moving in identically the same direction and in the same path. In (2), B4 stops and A5 runs into the back of him. This is a foul on A5. In this situation, the player behind is responsible for contact regardless of how abruptly the dribbler stops.

10-6-1 Number 32 leaps and attempts a jump shot. While No. 32 is airborne, No. 3 takes a position on the court to rebound. Number 32 returns to the court, and his momentum carries him into the back of No. 3 who had obtained a legal position. The foul in (3) is on No. 32, If the try is successful, the goal counts.

10-6-2 If No. 1 continues her course, she will commit a player-control charging foul. Because No. 1 has the ball, time and distance are of no consequence as No. 3 has obtained legal position by having both feet on the floor and facing No. 1.

10-6-2 Defensive player No. 5 may move into the path of a dribbler at any time, provided she is able to obtain a legal position. To initially obtain this position, she must be facing the dribbler with both feet on the floor. Subsequently, she may turn, crouch or retreat in order to avoid injury if he is charged by the dribbler. Number 5 has obtained a legal position. If she maintains her legal position, the dribbler is responsible for any contact.

10-6-2 Number 2 is running toward his basket but is looking back to receive an outlet pass. Number 3 has obtained a position in No. 2's path with both feet on the floor and facing the opponent. When No. 2 catches the ball and then runs into No. 3, it is a player-control foul. Once No. 2 has the ball, any contact with an opponent who is in legal position is No. 2's responsibility.

SCREENING PRINCIPLES

A screen is legal action by a player who, without causing contact, delays or prevents an opponent from reaching a desired position. The screener must be stationary, except when moving in exactly the same path and same direction as the opponent who is being screened. When stationary, the screener is not responsible for contact unless the screen is set outside the visual field of an opponent and so near that a stationary opponent makes contact on the first step. When the opponent is moving, the screen must be set far enough in advance of that opponent to permit him or her to stop or change direction. Two steps is the maximum.

When a screener causes slight contact with a defensive player, it usually takes the defense out of the play. In this case, slight contact should not be ruled incidental. On the other hand, when the defensive player in attempting to get around the screener causes contact that does not put the screener at a disadvantage, it should be ruled as incidental and ignored.

A player who is screened within his/her visual field is expected to avoid contact with the screener by stopping or going around the screener. In cases of blind screens, the opponent may make inadvertent contact with the screener. Such inadvertent contact is to be ruled incidental contact provided the opponent did all he/she could to minimize contact by stopping or attempting to stop or by changing directions, and provided the screener was not displaced if he or she had the ball.

It is very important that one official is looking off the ball as screens are being set there. Unless the entire play is seen it is impossible to make an accurate judgement as to which player is responsible for contact.

The following illustrations should be reviewed carefully as they show examples of some common screening situations. The basic principles must be thoroughly studied so that players understand them and official's calls are consistently correct.

10-6-3 Even though screener No. 5 positions herself too close to No. 4 for her to take one normal step back, there is no foul because there was no contact. A player cannot be charged with an illegal screen, or a blocking foul unless there has been contact.

TWO
STEPS

10-6-3 Number 3 has obtained a legal position. In obtaining a legal guarding position on a player without the ball, the guard must have both feet on the floor and must be facing the opponent. Time and distance must be sufficient to permit No. 4 to stop or change direction. The distance allowable is determined by the speed of No. 4. The distance never has to exceed two steps, regardless of how fast the opponent is moving.

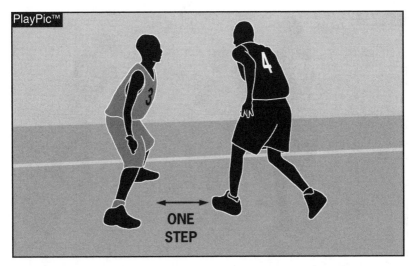

ONE
STEP

10-6-3 The foul will be on No. 3 if contact is made. When taking an initial defensive position in the path of the player who does not have the ball, time and distance must be sufficient to permit that player to stop or change his/her direction. When the player without the ball is moving rapidly, one step is not enough.

10-6-3 Legal screen as No. 10 and No. 12 set the screen to the side of No. 3, and the dribbler breaks around the screen without making contact. Legal play as the screen was set to the side of the defender.

10-6-3 A player screened from behind is given additional protection by the rules. When a stationary player is screened from behind, the screened player must be able to take a normal step backward without contacting the screener. The player being screened is not expected to see a screen set outside his/her visual field. Number 4 will be able to turn and see the screener and can either stop or go around her.

10-6-3 The defender attempts to force his way between No. 12 and No. 10 when there is not enough room. This is a charging foul on the defender. The screened player must stop on contact and/or go around the screeners rather than try to fight through the screen.

10-6-3 Number 12 fouls in (2) by stepping into No. 3's path as she attempts to go around the screen. The screener must be stationary and may not lean into the opponent or extend arms, elbows, hips, legs, etc. This illegal action is a blocking foul on No. 12.

10-6-3 A blocking foul on No. 15 who moved into the path of moving opponent No. 10 too late for him to stop or change direction. To set a screen on a moving opponent, the same principles on distance applies as when an initial guarding position is taken on a moving opponent without the ball. The opponent must be able to stop or change direction.

10-6-3 This is an example of a legal moving screen. There are not too many opportunities to use a legal moving screen. Number 10 may continue in the path he established at any speed he desires and any contact caused by No. 3 on No. 10 will be a charging foul on No. 3.

10-6-3 Number 12 screens at the side of stationary opponent No. 3. Number 12 is within No. 3's visual field and may be as close as she wishes without making contact. The defensive player can see the screen and, therefore, is expected to detour around it. The responsibility for contact is on No. 3.

Start Clock

Stop Clock

Stop Clock for
Jump/Held Ball

Stop Clock for Foul

Stop Clock for Foul
(Optional 'Bird Dog')

Directional Signal

Designated Spot

Visible Count

Beckon Substitute

60-Second Time-out

30-Second Time-out

No Score

Goal Counts

Point(s) Scored: Use 1 or 2 Fingers after signal 13

3-point Field Goal

Bonus Free Throw

Delayed Lane Violation

Traveling

Illegal Dribble

Over and Back or
Palming/Carrying Violation

Three-Second Violation

5-second Violation

10-second Violation

Free Throw, Designated
Spot or Other Violation

Excessively Swinging
Arm(s)/Elbow(s)

Kicking

Illegal Use of Hand

Hand Check

Holding

Blocking

Pushing or Charging

Player-Control Foul

Team-Control Foul

Intentional Foul

Double Foul

Technical Foul

Rules Books

Baseball • Basketball • Field Hockey • Football • Boys Gymnastics

Girls Gymnastics • Ice Hockey • Boys Lacrosse • Soccer • Softball

Spirit • Swimming and Diving/Water Polo

Track and Field/Cross Country • Volleyball • Wrestling

Published in **17 sports** by the National Federation of State High School Associations, Rules Books contain the official rules for high school athletic competition. These books are designed to explain all aspects of the game or contest. They are good for participants as well as coaches and contest officials.

The **NFHS** also publishes case books, manuals, handbooks and illustrated books in several sports to help in further explaining the rules.

For information on cost and shipping contact:
NATIONAL FEDERATION OF STATE HIGH SCHOOL ASSOCIATIONS
Customer Service Department
PO Box 361246
Indianapolis, IN 46236-5324
Phone: 1-800-776-3462
Fax: 317.899.7496
Order online: www.nfhs.com

NFHS ONLINE EDUCATIONAL SERVICES

Searchable NFHS Rules & Case Books

easy as...

 Go to www.nfhs.org

 Log in to secured area

 Search the rules

National Federation of State High School Associations
PO Box 690 | Indianapolis, IN 46206 | Phone: 317-972-6900 Fax: 317-822-5700

COACHES-OFFICIALS

MEMBERSHIP INFORMATION

NFHS Coaches Association – NFHS Officials Association

$30.00 ANNUAL DUES INCLUDES

ONE COACH AND ONE OFFICIAL SERVE ON EACH NFHS RULES COMMITTEE!

GENERAL LIABILITY INSURANCE

COACHES' OR OFFICIALS' QUARTERLY SUBSCRIPTION

AWARDS AND RECOGNITION!

→ **JOIN NOW** ←

NOTE: *DO NOT USE FOR CHEER/SPIRIT COACHES - REQUEST NFHS SPIRIT ASSOCIATION FORM FROM ADDRESS BELOW*

Mr/Mrs/Ms: _____ First Name: _____ M.I. _____

Last Name: _____ *(as it appears on your driver's license)*

Home Address: _____This is a new address ☐

City: _____ State/Province _____ Zip _____

Country: _____ Fax: ( ) _____

School/Organization Phone: ( ) _____ Home Phone: ( ) _____

For Insurance Purposes:

Social Security Number _____ Birthdate _____ ☐ Male ☐ Female

E-Mail Address: _____

Primary area of interest/expertise (sport) _____

First Year Officiating _____

First Year Coaching _____

I WORK PRIMARILY IN: *(Check only one)*
☐ High School Sports
☐ College Sports
☐ Youth League Sports

CHECK TYPE OF MEMBERSHIP

☐ **COACH** $30.00

☐ **OFFICIAL** $30.00

    (Residents of foreign countries add $9.00 mailing costs)

☐ Check ☐ VISA ☐ MasterCard ☐ American Express

DO NOT MAIL FORM WITHOUT PAYMENT
One annual payment provides member benefits for one year from the date payment is received by the NFHS.

Mail Payment to: NFHS
                    PO Box 690
                    Indianapolis, IN 46206

Account No.: _____ – _____ – _____ – _____

Exp. Date: _____ Card Security Code: _____

                  (call your merchant card provider for location of code.)

Cardholder Name _____

Signature _____

No purchase orders accepted   TOTAL AMOUNT ENCLOSED $_____

RULES PUBLICATIONS

Baseball Rules Book...................................$6.95	Girls Gymnastics Rules Book & Manual (2006-08)
Baseball Case Book $6.95	....$6.95
Baseball Umpires Manual (2007 & 2008) ..$6.95	Ice Hockey Rules Book............................$6.95
Baseball Simplified & Illustrated Rules $6.95	Boys Lacrosse Rules Book.......................$6.95
Baseball Rules by Topic $6.95	Soccer Rules Book...................................$6.95
Basketball Rules Book...............................$6.95	Softball Rules Book..................................$6.95
Basketball Case Book $6.95	Softball Case Book $6.95
Basketball Simplified & Illustrated Rules....$6.95	Softball Umpires Manual (2006 & 2007) ...$6.95
Basketball Officials Manual (2005-07).......$6.95	Spirit Rules Book $6.95
Basketball Handbook (2006-08)................$6.95	Swimming, Diving & Water Polo Rules Book
Basketball Rules by Topic.........................$6.95	....$6.95
Field Hockey Rules Book...........................$6.95	Track & Field Rules Book $6.95
Football Rules Book $6.95	Track & Field Case Book...........................$6.95
Football Case Book..................................$6.95	Track & Field Manual (2007 & 2008) $6.95
Football Simplified & Illustrated Rules $6.95	Volleyball Rules Book...............................$6.95
Football Handbook (2005 & 2006)............$6.95	Volleyball Case Book & Manual.................$6.95
Football Officials Manual (2006 & 2007)....$6.95	Wrestling Rules Book................................$6.95
Football Rules by Topic $6.95	Wrestling Case Book & Manual.................$6.95

MISCELLANEOUS ITEMS

NFHS Statisticians' Manual $6.50
Scorebooks: Baseball-Softball, Basketball, Swimming & Diving, Cross Country,
Soccer, Track & Field, Gymnastics, Volleyball, Wrestling and Field Hockey..............................$10.95
Diving Scoresheets (pad of 100)...$7.00
Volleyball Team Rosters & Lineup Sheets (pads of 100) $7.00
Libero Tracking Sheet...$7.00
Baseball/Softball Lineup Sheets - 3-Part NCR (sets/100) $8.50
Wrestling Tournament Match Cards (sets/100)..$7.00
Flipping Coin $5.50
NFHS Pin..$3.00
Competitors Numbers (Track and Gymnastics – Waterproof, nontearable,
black numbers and six colors of backgrounds
    Numbers are 1-1000 sold in sets of 100 ....$13.00/set
Lane Numbers (1-8), size 4" x 2 1/2"...$7.00/set

MISCELLANEOUS SPORTS ITEMS

High School Sports Record Book (2005)..$12.95	NFHS NEWS Binder $9.50
Court and Field Diagram Guide $19.95	High School Activities — A Community
NFHS Handbook (2006-07)...................... $9.00	Investment in America........................$79.95
Let's Make It Official................................. $5.00	Athletic Administration:
Guide for College-Bound Student-Athletes	A Comprehensive Guide $44.00
and Their Parents $2.00	Sports Medicine Handbook.....................$14.95

SPORTS VIDEO CASSETTES
Prices effective April 1, 2006 — March 31, 2007

SPORTS RULES 1/2" VHS VIDEO CASSETTES

17–MINUTE CASSETTES – $39.95

Baseball Rules Review

Basketball Rules Review

Football Rules Review

Girls Gymnastics Rules Review

Soccer Rules Update

Softball Rules Review

Spirit Rules Update

Spirit Rules for Dance/Drill Teams

Swimming & Diving Rules Review

Track & Field Rules Review

Volleyball Rules Review

Wrestling Rules Review

MISCELLANEOUS SPORTS VIDEO CASSETTES – $29.95

Baseball: Pitching By The Rules
Softball: Pitching By The Rules
Spirit: The Right Spirit
Track and Field: Vaulting Higher and Safer

MISCELLANEOUS SPORTS VIDEO CASSETTES – $24.95

Basketball: Blocking, Charging and Verticality
Basketball: Traveling and Dribbling

RULES UPDATE ON DVD – $15.95

High School Baseball: A Better Understanding of the Game

2006-07 NFHS ORDER BLANK

Name_____ Phone ( )_____

School and/or Organization _____

Address _____

| City | State | Zip |

(No PO Boxes. If charging order to a credit card please use address on card.)
If address has changed in the last year please fill in old address.

| Street | City | State | Zip |

Check one of the following: ☐ Visa ☐ MasterCard

Account No. _____ - _____ - _____ - _____ Exp. Date_____

Signature _____

P.O. # _____ (Order totals $50 or more)
(attach P.O.)

Item#	Description	Quantity	Unit Price	Total

SHIPPING & HANDLING CHARGES: If your subtotal is:

$10.00 to $15.00 ....add **$7.95**	$75.01 to $100.00 ...add **$15.95**
$15.01 to $25.00 ....add **$8.95**	$100.01 to $250.00 .add **$18.95**
$25.01 to $50.00 ....add **$9.95**	$250.01 to $500.00 .add **$21.95**
$50.01 to $75.00 .....add **$12.95**	Over $500.01 add 5% of subtotal

Second Day = Standard shipping charges plus **$15.00**
Overnight = Standard shipping charges plus **$25.00**
All shipments to Alaska, Hawaii, Virgin Islands and Canada – add **$10.00**
Call for charges outside continental U.S.
Minimum purchase on each order $10.00

Subtotal _____

Shipping & Handling Charge _____

TOTAL _____

Send to: **NFHS CUSTOMER SERVICE**
PO Box 361246, INDIANAPOLIS, IN 46236-5324
Phone 800-776-3462 or Fax 317.899.7496

ORDERING INFORMATION

PURCHASE ORDERS are welcomed but all orders under $50 must be prepaid. Purchase orders may be **either faxed or mailed** to our Customer Service office. If you mail a purchase order after it has been faxed to our Customer Service office, please note it is a **duplicate order**. All back-ordered items will be billed additional shipping charges. Terms net 30 days per invoice. All delinquent accounts are charged 1.5% finance charges. **PREPAID ORDERS** will be shipped upon receipt of completed order form accompanied by a check or money order. **All orders must include the proper amount for shipping and handling.**
*SHIPMENTS OUTSIDE UNITED STATES OR CANADA: Please write to NFHS headquarters for a quotation of total charges which will include a $2.00 surcharge and actual shipping charges. **Payment must be in U.S. dollars.** Please refer to www.nfhs.com to view our Return Policy.